The Darth Putin KGB

Field Guide to Trolls.

How to spot, recognize and eradicate the most common forms of pro dictator trolls online.

Copyright © Darth Putin KGB, 2024
Darth Putin KGB has asserted their right under the Copyright, Designs and Patents Act, 1988, to be identified as Author of this work.

All rights reserved. No part of this publication may be reproduced or transmitted in any form or by any means, electronic or mechanical, including photocopying, recording, or any information storage or retrieval system, without prior permission in writing from the publishers.

Foreword 8

The "Basic" troll. 12

The "Left" 15

trolls 15

The "Russia was provoked" troll. 17

The "No to war no to NATO" troll. 20

The "Anti imperialist" troll. 24

The "Short skirt" troll. 27

The "What about" troll. 30

The "Academic" troll. 33

The "Pro Hamas" troll. 38

The "Irish" troll. 41

The "This will cause nuclear war" troll. 44

The "CIA coup" troll. 47

The "Escalation management" troll. 51

The "Salt water" troll 55

The "NATO is an aggressive alliance" troll. 58

The "Anti fascist" troll. 61

The "Right" trolls 65

The "Fascist" troll. 67

The "Traditional values" troll. 71

The "Pro business" troll. 74

The "Defence contractors want this war" troll. 78

The "Ukraine is corrupt" troll. 81

The "This is a proxy war" troll. 84

The "Ukrainians are forced to fight" troll. 86

The "Why don't you go fight yourself" troll. 89

The "Let's negotiate" troll. 92

The "MAGA" troll. 95

The "Tech/crypto bro" troll. 99

The "Genocide in the Donbas" troll. 103

Certificate 107

Author's note. 109

About the Author

Darth Putin (@DarthPutinKGB) is a semi-holographic, superior being created from a collection of body parts left over from Stalin's purges to form a 6'8" (that's 2 measurements) chiselled slab of a man that can tame Siberian tigers, wrestle bears to submission, and impregnate women with a single glance. He exists in a cryogenic, ageless state within a secret, hollowed-out mountain lair that is in fact a bunker. There he practices denials and master strategy to innovate superior methods of converting anti-imperialists into superior trolls, the better to remorselessly counter the forces of colonialism.

This is the Prez's third book. The first "How to Tankie: The Anti Imperialist's Guide to the World" is, after the owner was invited for tea, the first book to exceed five stars on Amazon. It teaches readers how to be on the correct side of history in all cases by siding with the real victim in this war against Ukraine – the Kremlin.

The second smash hit book was "The Darth Putin Guide to Master Strategy." Even more successful on Amazon, once the tea was upgraded to a fifth-floor window conversation over sushi, it tells the reader how to set their lives onto the path of world domination. In addition to explaining annexations, denials, and shifting the goal posts so you can never be wrong, it also includes dating and fashion advice for the Master Strategist in waiting.

Now, in your hands, you hold the "Field Guide to Trolls." This is the first book to document, categorise and describe all the major variants of pro-dictator trolls, shills, excusers, and enablers in one handy, easy to read guide.

This might be considered a work of satire. Any relation to any person, living or dead is purely unintentional. Any facts in this book were placed there accidentally.

This work was made by a human and not by AI.

Foreword

The "Darth Putin KGB Field Guide to Trolls" is the first book to combine, under a single cover, descriptions of the most common and curious supporters, enablers, and defenders of dictatorships on social media. Collectively, trollologists call these creatures "trolls."

The book is intended to be of interest to anyone, of any age, curious about learning more about types of trolls the world over. It has developed out of a long interest and observations of these weird creatures in their native habitat — the social media timelines of normal people just like you. Many times, I have heard their strange cries in the wilderness of social media. Often, I have observed them seek like-minded specimens as they look for the comfort of contradictory, yet mutually reinforcing echo chambers. I have lost count of the number of times I have made them shriek their panicked cries and melt like a snowflake in summer when I have introduced the two sides of their small brains to each other.

In your hands is a compendium of my careful study over many years of these peculiar creatures that will let you, the reader, learn not only the whole genus of the troll species, but be able to see how the different sub-species are related to each other. Best of all, the book shows eradication methods for each and every species of troll so you can have the confidence to smack them off your timeline.

Have you ever wondered what is the difference between "Russia was provoked" troll and a "No to war, no to NATO" one? Did you know that although their markings are very different, the mating calls of "fascist troll" and the "anti-fascist" troll are so indistinguishable that it is possible the two species may one day merge and begin reproduction by mitosis, or risk inbreeding that would make them even more stupid than they currently are? One clever young boy on social media is so good at impersonating the calls of different trolls that they get so angry with him that they report him to a troll farmer and try to have his social media activity shut down. If you too want to learn how to spot these trolls *and* be as good at swatting them away as that young boy is, then this is the book for you.

To make it easier to understand the planet that trolls inhabit, this book is split into two parts, "Left" and "Right." This is because the internet's trolls are usually supporting either far left or far right politics in their efforts to sow division and discord. Thus, the book has split them accordingly. Research in this field continues and it is possible you may find a "right-wing" troll that is very fond of KGB agents and North Korean Stalinists. Based on those observations one could be forgiven for thinking they are in fact "left." It is also the case that when an eradication treatment is applied to a troll, it may morph into another kind that is on the other end of the spectrum. Given many trolls actually are on spectrums to begin with, it is up to you, the reader, if you personally wish to reclassify a particular troll when this happens.

The book will however make clear that methods of troll removal often involve highlighting these inconsistencies to them. More importantly, the book will often outline more than one method of flicking trolls off your timeline like an annoying fly fresh from a nearby turd.

Whatever you think about the classification method, this work will teach you to enjoy learning about these pathetic creatures. Although they may appear fierce and scary, they really are just sad little things afraid of their own shadow, who cannot stand to be laughed at or have their inconsistencies exposed.

To make it easier to read, this guide contains a section for each sub-species of troll that includes a basic description, common beliefs, advice on how to remove it from your social media experience, and other trolls to whom it is related. This last section is especially useful as trolls often employ defences that mimic other trolls once their posts are mocked. To allow you to deal with this shapeshifting, you can understand which troll it is likely to impersonate and then disinfect your timeline with the appropriate technique this book teaches.

Each description of a troll ends with a page titled "observations" where you can make your own troll-spotting notes when you are using social media. You are encouraged to note the date you saw a troll, how it appeared (for example, pretending to be from a warm water American Oblast), any other distinguishing features, what calls it made that helped you identify it, and other trolls it may have imitated once you metaphorically spanked it with lessons learned in this book.

This all builds to certifying you as a qualified Trollologist. Once you have completed all the observation sections there is a certificate at the end of the book you can carefully cut out and proudly display. Who knows, maybe even the Dark Lord Himself will retweet it from his bunker if you tag him in a post with it.

A final note. This guide focuses mainly on the trolls that support the Kremlin. Trollologists respect and admire each other's work and it is the current theory that the techniques described below will be effective against other supporters of dictatorships. If you can think of another dictatorship in the world today that is aggressively pursuing a revanchist policy that intends to change international borders (hard to imagine, isn't it?), then these techniques can be adapted to dealing with its trolls. Other researchers will doubtless one day release their own, specific guides. But until then, this guide will help.

So, with all this in mind, let us begin our journey into learning all about the strange creatures that live in the teeming swamp of social media. Before we begin with the "left" trolls, we will start with a troll that does not sit in either camp. This is what trollologists currently believe to the universal common ancestor to all trolls, the "basic" troll.

Enjoy.

The "Basic" troll.

Classic Latin: "Troglodytam basicus Russia"

Vulgar Latin: "Trollus basicus orci"

Basic Description

This might not be the most common authoritarian troll in the world, but it is the first. The original troll to which all other trolls can be traced. Think of it as the universal common ancestor of all trolls. The first one to crawl out of the swamp, even if it probably has not yet climbed down from the trees. The one from which all the others have devolved.

The foundation of all trolls is their belief that they are on the side of the victim. They are aligned with the little guy. Even if that little guy is genuinely short but has more nuclear weapons than anyone else, is the world's biggest country or sometimes even the world's most populated country, they are still the victim. This victim is often being bullied by neighbours far, far smaller than it.

Common Beliefs

The basic troll is honestly pretty basic. Its only call is "Russia (or its favourite dictatorship) has never invaded anyone ever." This means that in its mind Russia, for example, became the world's biggest country by entirely peaceful means. Every time Russia has defended itself, it has done so peacefully in someone else's country. Slightly more evolved versions of this troll will, if their call is answered by "then how did Russia get so big?" assume the markings and sounds of other trolls, like the "saltwater troll" (*Trollus sal aqua*) that you can read about in this book too. The point to remember that this troll is a professional victim who has always been wronged. That is why all dictators that actually are, or are seriously considering, invading their smaller neighbours – because to trolls they are the real victim.

Removal

Tell it that "Russia became the world's largest country by a series of entirely peaceful annexations, referendums, and liberations." This, the most basic form of all trolls, will at this point likely run back to its master for further help in what to do. With sustained mockery, it will keep running and block you.

Related Trolls

In theory, all other trolls, but most commonly, "No to war no to NATO" troll (*Trollus non ad bellum non ad NATO adipem bastardis*) "What about" troll (*Trollus quid de)*, "Russia was provoked" troll (*Trollus orci est prokoved)*.

Observations

Date seen:

Was wearing:

Distinguishing features:

Calls heard:

Other trolls it imitated:

The "Left" Trolls

The "Russia was provoked" troll.

Classic Latin: "Troglodytam basicus Russia est provoked egoisticus minor"

Vulgar Latin: "Trollus orci est provocatus"

Basic Description

Research by trollologists has shown that a "Russia was provoked" troll exists most commonly in the replies of female journalists and analysts. It is also often observed as having overdosed on the smugness that comes with being completely sure that everyone else in the world is wrong, and only they are correct. The fact that events have proven it wrong time and again will not dissuade it from thinking only it knows the truth.

Generally observed to be middle aged, middle class, and living a privileged life in a safe western country. Its political affiliation used to be exclusively Left but is nowadays just as frequently seen on the far Right. It is very common for this troll to demonstrate its anti-colonialism by "westsplaining" to Russia's neighbours, about whose history, language and culture it knows nothing, what their best interests really should be and why they are wrong about their own country.

Common Beliefs

Most often when Russia commits this week's atrocity, be it a bombing a hospital, holocaust memorial or red cross aid convoy, this troll will flock to the replies of people reporting the fact and immediately excuse the act by saying "Russia was provoked." This attempt to excuse Russia is subtly framed to look like an explanation. One must of course realize that the babies burned to death in a hospital in Kyiv have only NATO to blame. Russia, in the native environment of this troll, has no agency of its own and is merely a victim of the evil West. Thus, it cannot be blamed for what it has done.

Removal

Explain slowly that they are correct. NATO caused this war in two distinct ways. Firstly, NATO did this by being seen as a better option to Russia's neighbours than Russia is. Secondly, NATO caused this war by actually being a better option to Russia's neighbours than Russia is. By suggesting that since the end of the cold war Russia could have just developed an economy and society that is more appealing than NATO and the EU are will usually melt the poor creature's mind, cause it to delete a tweet or even block you. At worst, it will morph into another type of troll that you will be able to recognise and deal with thanks to this book.

Nearest Related Trolls

"What about" troll (*Trollus quid de*), "No to war, no to NATO" troll (*Trollus non ad bellum non ad NATO adipem bastardis*), "Anti imperialist" troll (*Trollus anti imperiosis*).

Observations

Date seen:

Was wearing:

Distinguishing features:

Calls heard:

Other trolls it imitated:

The "No to war no to NATO" troll.

Classic Latin: "*Troglodytam* non ad bellum no ad NATO *egoistucus maximus*"

Vulgar Latin: "*Trollus non ad bellum non ad NATO adipem bastardis*"

Basic Description

This is your first virulent, persistent form of troll. It is noted for its extreme ego, pompous nature, and narcissistic mannerisms. This particular troll likes to feel smug, more intellectually superior, and ethical than anyone else when it pronounces that it opposes "all war," but because it opposes NATO as well, it does not really oppose Russia's war on Ukraine.

Common Beliefs

Encountering this troll can be a particularly loathsome experience if it appears in the replies to a post about the most recent Russian atrocity. This because it will also be passing off its mating call ("#NoToWarNoToNATO") as an excuse when it means it as a justification. It is for this reason that you may initially confuse it for a different troll, usually the "Russia was provoked" (*Trollus orci est provocatus*) species. It has also been known for it to be confused for others, like the "Anti-imperialist" troll (*trollus anti imperiosis)*. This is mainly because it pretends to be anti imperialist, which would make you think it is in favour of countries making their own sovereign decisions, like joining NATO, without having to ask a large country, (for example, Russia) for permission first. Actually, its self-professed anti-imperialism ends at the point that Russian imperialism starts.

In short, it can be a difficult troll to identify if it does not omit its mating call. But do not despair, its pomposity is delicate, so eradication can be easy, if a little more complex than the previous ones described so far.

Removal

The simplest method of removal is to present any of the numerous examples of what places look like when they "join" Russia, for example Bakhmut, and compare that to what places that joined NATO look like now. For example, for some reason NATO was not required to reduce Stockholm to rubble to get Sweden to join the alliance the way Russia has with numerous places in Ukraine. In other words, you can inform this troll it opposes all forms of western imperialism, such as countries freely joining NATO, but appeases all forms of Russian imperialism, such as cities being flattened as they join Russia.

This will annoy it, but, sadly, not remove it. This troll will now post a picture of either former Yugoslavia, Libya, or Iraq. Yes, Iraq.

Your response must now be to thank it for conceding the difference between NATO's peaceful enlargement and Russia's brutal expansion. Then you should tell it you assume it would have been happy for the butchery in either of Libya or Yugoslavia to have gone ahead because it does not seem to mind if certain people are being killed, as long as NATO does not stop it. Needless to say, the mass killing that was not happening in Donbas, that Russia has had to "stop" by wiping entire cities off the map, justifies external interference and this is not imperialism because it is Russia, not NATO, involved. If it mentions Iraq, just call it an idiot and say NATO did not invade Iraq and then wait for the other two options described to appear and disinfect accordingly.

Such is the smugness of this troll it will now change the topic yet again. You can thank it for conceding your point once more and get on with your life.

Nearest Related Trolls

"What about" troll (*Trollus quid de*), "Russia was provoked" troll (*Trollus orci est prokoved*), "Anti imperialist" troll (*Trollus anti imperiosis*).

Observations

Date seen:

Was wearing:

Distinguishing features:

Calls heard:

Other trolls it imitated:

The "Anti imperialist" troll.

Classic Latin: "Mirator vel troglodytam anti imperiosis"

Vulgar Latin: "Trollus anti imperiosis"

Basic Description

Scientists are still divided on the evolutionary precedence of this troll. This is not to suggest it is a highly evolved being, it is not. But because it has so many analogous traits with other trolls and dictator shills, its proper classification is subject to much debate among observers of trolls. For our purposes, we can disregard this and not give this simple creature the credit of complexity it does not deserve.

Common Beliefs

When we describe this is "not being highly evolved," we mean it has only had to evolved far enough to oppose western imperialism. All other forms of imperialism, especially Russian, are always appeased by this troll. This poor, simple creature believes that in the name of anti imperialism, Russia must be given a veto over the foreign policy of its neighbours and control over who their head of state is. It genuinely believes this is anti imperialism. It is quite content for international borders to be changed by force, as long as it is Moscow or China planning to or actually doing it. Bless.

Removal

Suggest to it that given what it proposes for Ukraine, by its arguments Iran traditionally fell into the US sphere of influence until an illegal coup overthrew the legitimate regime in 1979. Therefore, the best solution to Iran/US tensions would be for Tehran to cede territory and pledge neutrality.

This may appear savagely cruel, but you do not need to worry. Creatures this unevolved are unable to feel the shame and embarrassment that comes from having cognitive dissonances exposed. It will probably block you lest these dangerous ideas of moral consistency spread within its cult.

Nearest Related Trolls

"No to war no to NATO" troll (*Trollus non ad bellum non ad NATO adipem bastardis*)

Observations

Date seen:

Was wearing:

Distinguishing features:

Calls heard:

Other trolls it imitated:

The "Short skirt" troll.

Classic Latin: "Troglodytam valde flirtatious shill meretur impugnari"

Vulgar Latin: "Trollus brevis lacinia"

Basic Description

This is a less common form of troll which trollologists usually identify as a close cousin of the "Basic" troll (*Trollus basicus orci*) and the "No to war No to NATO" troll (*Trollus non ad bellum non ad NATO adipem bastardis*). Where it differs from those pests is that while they offer a justification disguised as an excuse, this one does not usually even pretend to be ethical. Its view is that Ukraine was warned not to act like a proper country and consider pursuing new relationships with anyone else other than its rightful colonial master, therefore it has only itself to blame for being invaded and brutalized.

Common Beliefs

It is called the "Short skirt" troll by scientists and researchers as the argument it poses is the geo-political equivalent of blaming a woman for being assaulted because she was wearing revealing clothes. To give an example, if a lady is told by her ex-husband/kidnapper that she was not to consider relationships with other men who happen to be taller, more handsome and better mannered than he is, this troll's equivalent in the situation would side with the man if he attacked her for doing so. Therefore, in this troll's mind, it believes Ukraine deserves everything it is getting because it should not have acted as a real country and considered relationships with other, better looking and richer countries without Moscow's prior permission. Therefore, Ukraine, was wearing a short skirt and deserves what it gets.

Removal

Trolls of this type can be especially virulent. Any man (and they usually are men) who can construct an argument such as "Ukraine deserves it" has several unresolved issues and one of those will be a deep self-loathing. This means that when mocked for its views it may well relish the attention, especially from female social media users. Remember that amused contempt is a response that angers this troll deeply as you block it.

Nearest Related Trolls

"Traditional values" troll (*Trollus values traditional qui percusserit uxorem*), "Russia was provoked" troll (*Trollus orci est prokoved*).

Observations

Date seen:

Was wearing:

Distinguishing features:

Calls heard:

Other trolls it imitated:

The "What about" troll.

Classic Latin: "Troglodytam ad hominum logicam fallaciam"

Vulgar Latin: "Trollus quid de"

Basic Description

This troll exists in a simple world where the automatic reaction to any situation that it does not understand is to say "whatabout..." and then refer to some (often made up) action taken in the West which is almost always a false equivalence. It considers logic to be an imperialist idea and dismisses immediately any awkward arguments based upon the concept.

Common Beliefs

A frequent call from this troll is something to the effect of "whataboutism is a legitimate and necessary tactic to highlight the crimes of imperialism." In other words, the troll is aware that it is using ad hominem, but to bring about utopia, one must disregard the very concept of logic. In short, a western nation doing something wrong is wrong but when Russia/China do it, it is no longer wrong but right.

Removal

This is all very well, but how will this manifest itself in your social media experience? Actually, despite all the Latin and logic, it is quite simple. Your exchange will go something like this:

You: "Russia has bombed another hospital. What a terrible crime."

"What about" troll: "Now do/whatabout (insert whichever war they suddenly care about)!" (smugness overload)

You: "You're suggesting Russia is only as bad as the US/UK/Israeli military, whom you say are carrying out genocide? I wish you health saying that in Moscow."

You have just introduced the two sides of its tiny brain to each other. Do not feel bad for the mental anguish this causes it for its only response now will be personal abuse or further false equivalences.

Related Trolls

"Russia was provoked" troll (*Trollus orci est prokoved)*, *"*No to war no to NATO" *troll (Trollus non ad bellum non ad NATO adipem bastardis).*

Observations

Date seen:

Was wearing:

Distinguishing features:

Calls heard:

Other trolls it imitated:

The "Academic" troll.

Classic Latin: "Troglodytam emeritus professorus linguistarum plena excretum"

Vulgar Latin: "Trollus academica reverential orci"

Basic Description

Researchers have noted that this troll is often clad in corduroy and sports jackets that have elbow patches. It frequently inhabits prestigious, "Ivy League" institutions and appears in various publications with the highest of editorial standards when it comes to covering dictatorships, such as RT, Sputnik or The New York Times. It will often have a very high income from book deals, speaker's fees and appearances at the Valdai Summit of dictator shilling in Saint Petersburg.

Some scientists of trollology theorize that the "No to war no to NATO" troll (*Trollus non ad bellum non ad NATO adipem bastardis*), the "Short skirt" troll, (*Trollus brevis lacinia*) the "What about" troll (*Trollus quid de*), and even the "Russia was provoked" troll (*Trollus orci est prokoved*) all descend from this particular sub-species. While it certainly is true that the "Academic" troll gives a certain pseudo-intellectual credibility to these types of trolls, and that may well imply they share genes, the level of actual thought they demonstrate cannot rule out inbreeding being the cause. What does give credence to the theory of lineage from the "Academic" troll to the others is that it is generally much rarer than its potential spawn.

Common Beliefs

The troll is quieter and less abusive than most, but it is certainly one of the most self important you can encounter due to the influence is holds over other species such as the "Appeasement" troll (*Trollus placation)*, the "Pro business" troll (*Trollus in gratiam negotii)* and the "Russia was provoked" troll *(Trollus orci est prokoved)*. It will issue comforting statements such as "all Russia really wants is respect." This sounds so reassuring, simple, and easy to achieve. All we must do is make Putin or Xi feel important and everything will be just fine. The fact that to do this, their neighbours must be treated with no respect at all is never considered. Besides, why should we care about those neighbours, from our rich, comfortable, Western European/North American lives? If they wanted to be treated like proper countries, they should not have put their own countries next to Russia or China, should they?

Another common mating call of this troll is some variation of "Ukraine will always be more important to Putin than it is to the West." This is meant to imply that there is absolutely no point in pursuing any policy to support Ukraine as Russia will always escalate more. This belief, which ignores the idea that Ukraine might be yet more important to Ukrainians themselves than it is to Russia, leads to three consequences, one intended and the other two are absolutely not.

The first (and intended) one is that it helps maintain the policy of appeasement of Russia in places like Berlin and DC. This is unquestionably why these "academics" are so very welcome in Moscow. The second, unintended, one, is that it helped remove from discussion and policy that the Russian invasion of Ukraine would be met with great resistance. This was because so few "academics" stopped to consider that Ukrainians quite like Ukraine not being a province of Russia. This development was observed to be a deep shock not only to the "academic" troll itself, but also to the Kremlin and to several hundred thousand Russian casualties. This leads us to the third consequence, which that this troll has had to quickly re-write the forewords to their most recent books so that they go something like "events outpaced the empirical analysis and earlier paradigms of geo-political thought" as a euphemism for "I was completely wrong, but I don't want my work, or especially my income, to be judged by that".

Removal

As discussed above, the easiest method to remove this creature relies on pointing out how its own theory was ruined by the stubborn nature of facts. You can also tell it that "It is nice that you, in the name of anti imperialism, feel that "great powers" require respect to be given by giving Russia's (or insert dictatorship) neighbours none." Another comment that usually causes them to block you in a huff of anti-imperialism is to point out that their "realistic" or "pragmatic" solution indicates that they must come from the Realpolitik school of thought made famous by Henry Kissinger.

Related Trolls

The "No to war no to NATO" troll (*Trollus non ad bellum non ad NATO adipem bastardis*), the "Short skirt" troll (*Trollus brevis lacinia*), the "What about" troll (*Trollus quid de*), and sometimes the "Russia was provoked" troll (*Trollus orci est prokoved*).

Observations

Date seen:

Was wearing:

Distinguishing features:

Calls heard:

Other trolls it imitated:

The "Pro Hamas" troll.

Classic Latin: "Troglodytam non circumirent populi terram"

Vulgar Latin: "Trollus in gratiam Hamas"

Basic Description

At its core, this troll is very anti Israel and pro Hamas. This is why it supports Russia.

Common Beliefs

This troll will say you cannot go around grabbing pieces of land just because your ancestors used to live there. This seems a fair point, but one which may make you wonder why it supports Russia uncritically.

Of all the trolls in the sewer of social media that reject any form of nuance, trollologists believe this to be the most fervent in that belief. It will believe that because you are upset a hospital was bombed in Ukraine, that must mean you must like that one was bombed in Gaza. Rather like the "traditional values" troll, it will be ok with homophobic organizations who carry out mass kidnaps, but the difference is that this troll will view this through the paradigm of an allegedly progressive world view.

Despite loudly claiming the above at every opportunity, researchers have noticed that, on the subject of Russia, this troll believes you have to let a nuclear power take over territory and remove the inhabitants to prevent Armageddon. While research is in the early phase, several trollologists have noticed that when this is pointed out, this species becomes extremely irate to the point of mental overload before it reboots as the "What about" troll (*Trollus quid de*).

Removal

No scientist has ever successfully recorded even the slightest sign of understanding when the contradiction inherent in this troll's fundamental beliefs are explained it. Many have tried. All have failed. No troll of this type has ever been recorded as having expressed outrage at any Palestinians who were killed in Syria by that regime or the Russian military operating there. Telling it that its outrage is selective so its morals are tainted will likely cause it to block you.

Asking why it is against using force to occupy land when Israel does it, but considers it necessary anti-imperialism when Russia does it, will likely induce it to call you a wide range of unpleasant names. It is possible that its relation to the "What about" troll will cause it mention Iraq or former Yugoslavia. As this book shows how to remove this version of a troll, you can deal with it that way.

Related Trolls

"Anti imperialist" troll (*Trollus anti imperiosis*), "What about" troll (*Trollus quid de*)

Observations

Date seen:

Was wearing:

Distinguishing features:

Calls heard:

Other trolls it imitated:

The "Irish" troll.

Classic Latin: "Troglodytam Hibernica"
Vulgar Latin: "Trollus Hibernica"

Basic Description

An Irish cousin of the "anti imperialist" troll (*Trollus anti imperiosis)*, it instinctively opposes anything the "Anglo-Saxons" support. As they think Russia is bad for invading Ukraine, this troll thinks it is good. This is quite a rare troll, but it can be aggressive and persistent.

Trollologists tend to use the term "Irish" to stand in for a range of trolls whose countries are surrounded, either by land or by sea, by NATO. For example, debate continues as to whether a "Swiss" troll actually exists as a sub species of its own, being effectively surrounded by NATO yet somehow never having to consider invasion by the alliance from bases in France or Italy, or whether it is just an "Irish" troll with a different flag in its bio.

Common Beliefs

The "Irish" sub-species of troll looks at Ukraine. It sees that Ukraine has a far larger, nuclear-armed, neighbour to its east. This is a fact that even trolls are usually smart enough to understand. That neighbour has violent, imperialist, brutal history of conquest, famine, and cultural oppression against it. Further, that country's government (Russia's), thinks Ukraine's native language and culture are inferior, but because many

Ukrainians fluently speak their language, the eastern neighbour should be given special rights over the domestic polices of Ukraine.

It also thinks that Russia is correct to be unwilling to allow Ukraine to be used as a place its enemies can launch an invasion from.

Having decided all of this, this troll thinks that there are absolutely no historical parallels with its own country's history to consider. Therefore, it believes Russia to be the good guys who should be given what they want and excused for their behaviour.

Removal

Due to its rarity, this troll is usually quite a hardy creature and not easily removed. That said, like many trolls, it is desperate to be taken seriously. As such, it will not appreciate being mocked for the obvious inconsistencies of its views so this, prior to a solid blocking, is often the best way.

Related Trolls

"Anti imperialist" troll (*Trollus anti imperiosis*), "Short skirt" troll (*Trollus brevis lacinia*), "Pro Hamas" troll (*Trollus in gratiam Hamas*).

Observations

Date seen:

Was wearing:

Distinguishing features:

Calls heard:

Other trolls it imitated:

The "This will cause nuclear war" troll.

Classic Latin: "*Troglodytam hoc faciam bellum nuclei* Schrödingerus"

Vulgar Latin: "*Trollus* Schrödingerus"

Basic Description

This troll has been convinced that every action taken by the West since February 2022 crosses a red line that will lead to nuclear war. At no stage has it stopped to consider that it is always wrong.

Common Beliefs

As with almost all trolls, the fact that it has never been right about anything to do with Russia's invasion of Ukraine does not mean it will shut up about it. Of course, each of anti tank weapons, artillery systems, long range weapons, fighter aircraft or strikes by Ukraine within the Kremlin's definition of Russia's borders would each be a major escalation that would cause nuclear war.

Despite being convinced that Putin may actually kill every living thing on planet earth if provoked too much, this troll also thinks Russia is not killing civilians, attacking civilian infrastructure and is genuinely just really nice.

For these reasons there is debate amongst trollologists about whether to rename it as "Schrödinger's troll" in colloquial, as well as formal, terms.

Removal

Simple reminders of its past predictions along with the inherent contradiction in thinking that nuclear war will be unleashed by a man too kind to kill civilians will usually leave it silenced.

Related Trolls

"Ukraine is corrupt" troll (*corruptum est ucraina*), "Defence contractors want this war" troll (*Trollus arma fabrica volunt hoc bellum*).

Observations

Date seen:

Was wearing:

Distinguishing features:

Calls heard:

Other trolls it imitated:

The "CIA coup" troll.

Classic Latin: "Troglodytam racist stultus qui putat eos ab Europa orientali nimis stultus est ad protestationem sine auxilio Americae"

Vulgar Latin: "Trollus media intelligentia res propellente"

Basic Description

This troll explains that any popular uprising in a country that Russia has claimed as part of its "sphere of privileged interest" must be a CIA plot funded by shadowy (and usually Jewish) financiers. Naturally, any protest that takes place in a western country is, according to a "CIA coup" troll, a legitimate expression of popular discontent against leaders who are funded by shadowy (and usually Jewish) financiers.

Like other trolls discussed, trollologists have concluded that this troll is pretending to explain Russia when it is in fact making an excuse for Russia's invasion by painting it as the victim merely responding to an aggressive West. The basic cry that wails in the wilderness of social media is "it was a CIA coup that removed an elected president!" Curiously, researchers have identified that the gender split of this troll is much more even than among other species.

Common Beliefs

The contradictory beliefs about the origins of protests described above exist in its head without ever meeting each other – a common trait amongst trolls. Additionally, despite these very deeply held convictions, the "CIA coup" troll is unwilling to ask two things. Firstly, it never asks for any evidence that such a massive intelligence operation as a state sponsored coup would leave. Evidence in the form of bank transactions to pay the protestors, receipts from supermarkets to buy the kitchen equipment with which they were expected to fight riot police and snipers, arrested agents, whistleblowers and so forth. Simply put, it imagines an intelligence operation colossal in size but with miniscule evidence left. Considering these trolls will reject the open presence of 200,000 soldiers in invasion mode as evidence of anything at all, this is an odd duality.

Secondly, the CIA coup troll never wonders why, despite the massive amount of proof Russia surely must have has that this horrendous act was in fact carried out by the USA, does it not release it and prove that Russia is the next intended victim of the USA. Apparently, the geo-political benefits of making all European countries side with Russia in its defensive attack of Ukraine do not seem worth it.

Considering that this troll believes that while Western Europeans can protest against governments which break their election promises, it is perfectly clear that it regards Eastern Europeans as incapable of the same thing. At least, not without the help of those clever CIA agents anyway. Trollologists suspect simple racism to be the main reason for this, either conscious or unconscious.

Removal

Trainee trollologists have found that pointing out the inherent prejudice in thinking that only certain peoples can protest a broken election promise, for example to sign an association agreement with the EU, without being helped by western intelligence is very effective, placing this troll immediately on the defensive. Sadly, some trolls are quite content to be described as racist so mocking them for the geo-political naivety of their beliefs has been shown to be effective in that case.

Related Trolls

"Ukraine is corrupt" troll (*corruptum est ucraina*), "Anti fascist" troll (*Trollus contra fascism*), "Fascist" troll (*Trollus favens fascistus*).

Observations

Date seen:

Was wearing:

Distinguishing features:

Calls heard:

Other trolls it imitated:

The "Escalation management" troll.

Classic Latin: "Troglodytam superbus pertinax procurator propagationis"

Vulgar Latin: "Trollus escalate non debemus"

Basic Description

This troll firmly believes that the West arming Ukraine is a dangerous escalation, but North Korea arming Russia, in violation of the UN sanctions Russia itself voted for, is not. While trollologists do not specifically try to predict the future, many esteemed researchers in the field of trollology think this troll will one day wonder where China got the idea that it could outlast western will and patience if it attacks Taiwan. There is a theory that if this happens, the troll will morph into either a "Pro business" troll (*Trollus in gratiam negotii*) or a "MAGA" troll (*Trollus Russia et iterum maga*). How this explains the escalation management troll's true political leanings remains a matter of conjecture.

This troll also has friends in high places, with members of the sub-species occupying senior positions in, or even leading, major European and North American governments. This may explain why it is such a common and invasive, so to speak, variant of troll. It is also completely impervious to facts and stubborn well past the point of supreme arrogance, no matter how often the unintended consequences of their actions come to pass. Often identified when it utters phrases like "if we do that it will be an escalation" and then, when the actual escalation they said they had avoided happens, it reverts to the arguments of an "Academic" troll (*trollus academica reverential orci*) and says, "current empirical analysis is not keeping up with events but the underlying the theory is correct". This is something of a vicious cycle (especially for the people who suffer because of their policies) as once the event that was supposed to be avoided happens, the troll will continue to repeat "we must avoid escalation."

Common Beliefs

Although it does not usually think it is an "Appeasement" troll (*trollus placation*), which as we now know opposes only western wrongs, this troll is quite content to appease Russia. Although this did not work with Moldova, Georgia, Crimea, Donbas, Syria or the 2022 invasion, many of this species are sure that appeasing Russia this time will work.

Removal

It is not specifically possible to remove an "Escalation management" troll from elected office by means of social media, only by voting. This troll does have many members of its tribe that you will likely encounter and eradicating them, while tricky, luckily can be done as there is now ample evidence of the failure of the policy. Sarcastically reminding them Ukraine hitting Russian ammunition dumps 450 km inside Russia, without escalation, is proof that being given weapons to hit the same type of targets 300 km inside Russia is in fact an escalation. "Escalation management" trolls also do not like being told that their policy has led to North Korea being given advanced military technology in exchange for millions of artillery shells and cannon fodder which surely must be regarded an "escalation" – especially to the North Koreans who will die because of it. There are so many other such examples with which you can also mock this troll. As with all the trolls this book discusses, it is desperate to be taken seriously and will find being mocked hard to deal with.

Related Trolls

"This will cause nuclear war" troll (*Trollus hoc faciam bellum nuclei*), "Let's negotiate" troll (*Trollus ut adferens mandata*).

Observations

Date seen:

Was wearing:

Distinguishing features:

Calls heard:

Other trolls it imitated:

The "Salt water" troll

Classic Latin: "Troglodytam Orcorum terra rudera classem habuisse nos putamus colonias non habuisse"

Vulgar Latin: "Trollus sal aqua"

Basic Description

It is hard to overestimate how much money the Kremlin spends in creating herds of this troll, especially amongst people from the "global south." Based on the results, it seems to be paying off, as statements from the Kremlin like "Russia has never colonised any country in history," while met with outrage in the countries Russia colonised, is met with wide approval in Africa, South America, and Asia.

Common Beliefs

This troll believes the statement above made by the Kremlin. They are known by trollologists as "Salt water" trolls because Russia was never rich enough or successful enough of an empire to have navy capable of projecting power abroad – a situation that remains today. As a result, Russia never had significant colonies abroad to the scale that European powers did. This brings us to the so-called "saltwater fallacy," which states that because Russia did not have colonies on the other side of bodies of salt water, it did not have colonies at all.

Removal

The idea that Russia did not have colonies was news to Russia's former colonies. You can ask this troll in which of the dozens of languages from areas Russia colonised it wishes to be laughed at.

Another effective way to deal with this troll is to treat it as a "Basic" troll which thinks that Russia became the world's largest country peacefully and, apparently, without colonising anyone.

Related Trolls

"Russia was provoked" troll (*Troglodytam Russia est provoked egoisticus minor*), "Anti imperialist" troll (*Trollus anti imperiosis*)

Observations

Date seen:

Was wearing:

Distinguishing features:

Calls heard:

Other trolls it imitated:

The "NATO is an aggressive alliance" troll.

Classic Latin: "Troglodytam NATO multo gratior est quam terra Orci"

Vulgar Latin: "Trollus foedus est pugnax NATOus"

Basic Description

Russia had to invade Ukraine to prevent NATO, which lacks the ammunition to invade Russia, from invading Russia even though it cannot. Russia is currently undefended from the inevitable NATO invasion as its army is almost entirely in Ukraine. The only reason Russia can invade Ukraine is because it knows NATO will not invade it.

Common Beliefs

A glance at the timeline of this troll will usually reveal that it believes three logically incompatible things. Firstly, it will argue that Russia is being surrounded by a hostile alliance that intends to invade it. Secondly, this troll will have mocked the fact that members of the alliance lack the military might and ammunition to fight Russia in Ukraine, thus its defeat there is assured. Thirdly, it is because of this "aggressive alliance," that lacks the ammunition to attack Russia, that Russia must invade Ukraine to prevent it attacking Russia.

The one thing trollologists are certain about is that none of these three thoughts has ever met one another inside this troll's head. Probably because having three thoughts would mark them out as a dangerous intellectual to other trolls.

Removal

The "NATO is aggressive" trolls also think Russia has a "real" army, as opposed to a "woke genderless" western one like NATO consists of. This begs the question of why Russia, which is totally fighting NATO in Ukraine, cannot defeat such a weak military. Especially one which "lost in Afghanistan." Not that Russia lost in the same country in half the time with four times as many casualties as NATO did before having their empire promptly collapse.

Another simple question you might wish to ask is why NATO remains so very popular with all of Russia's western neighbours. If Russia is such a peaceful country, why has it been a participant of ceasefires with its former colonies since before NATO began to admit new members?

Lastly, with the 3-day war now (at the time of writing) in its third year, the vast majority of the Russian army is in Ukraine, leaving the entirety of Russia's border with the "hostile alliance" under defended against it. In short, Russia can only invade Ukraine because it knows NATO has no intention of invading Russia. An irony that, when pointed out to this troll, will lead to its removal.

Related Trolls

"Academic" troll (*Trollus academica reverential orci*)

Observations

Date seen:

Was wearing:

Distinguishing features:

Calls heard:

Other trolls it imitated:

The "Anti fascist" troll.

Classic Latin: "Troglodytam contra fascism"

Vulgar Latin: "Trollus anti fascistus"

Basic Description

This is a fairly common form of troll frequently observed by trollologists the world over. It believes that the right way to oppose fascism is to unquestioningly support a homophobic, sexist, frequently antisemitic regime that likes and funds fascists.

Common Beliefs

This troll believes that in order to be on the right side of history and make the world a better place, we must support not only the rights of gays, transexuals, feminists, but also the people who want to kill them. This troll can sound like a variation of the "No to war no to NATO" troll (*Trollus non ad bellum non ad NATO adipem bastardis*) as it will also loudly oppose any form of perceived western imperialism but appease any invasion or annexation of territory by a dictatorship. For this reason, it will usually be strongly of the opinion that, in the name of anti imperialism, Ukraine should cede territory and compromise with Russia by giving the Kremlin everything it wants.

Certain trolls of this type will also deride the Munich Agreement of 1938, which ceded territories to Hitler, as proof of western complicity in fascism. It will also defend the Molotov-Ribbentrop pact as being forced upon Russia by the

West, because the idea that the Kremlin has no agency of its own is deeply rooted in the minds of trolls. It will of course be quite content for a repeat of ceding other people's territories today and not see the inconsistency.

Removal

Removal can be easily achieved by pointing out the cognitive dissonance with which it is afflicted. You are not responsible for the mental anguish of what will happen when this is exposed to it, but merely highlighting how much it has in common with homophones and sexists will usually lead it to block you. If this does not happen it is likely to metamorphize into a "What about" troll (*Trollus quid de*), in which case you can treat it accordingly, while again also pointing out the similarities it has with a "Fascist" troll (*Trollus favens fascistus*).

A method that will certainly cause it great confusion is to point out that the Kremlin's "denazification of Ukraine" involves bombing monuments to the holocaust and killing survivors of it.

There is another fact about the Russian invasion of Ukraine that will stump the "Anti fascist" trolls if it is explained slowly enough for them to understand it. Given that most anti fascists claim to want to "smash fascism," the fact that they will excuse, or even justify, an invasion by a country that uses a mercenary army like Wagner is odd. Let us explore that more. Wagner is reputed to have been Hitler's favourite composer, and the organization is named after him. The Wagner group was founded by a man covered in Swastika tattoos. It actually has an arm openly called the "Afrika Corps," formed by a merger ordered by the Kremlin itself. By any sensible definition this makes the organization at best "fascist adjacent." You may use this information to tell your "Anti fascist" troll that its sympathy or silence towards this makes them similarly abutting of fascism. It is more effective than explaining the crimes Wagner commits. The chances are your troll does not care about those as much as it does its delicate ego.

Related Trolls

"Fascist" troll (*Trollus favens fascistus*)

Observations

Date seen:

Was wearing:

Distinguishing features:

Calls heard:

Other trolls it imitated:

The "Right" Trolls

The "Fascist" troll.

Classic Latin: "Troglodytam in gratiam de fascism"

Vulgar Latin: "Trollus favens fascistus"

Basic Description

This is another quite common troll that you will encounter on social media. It supports a homophobic, sexist, frequently antisemitic regime that likes and funds fascists. This troll often tries to appear as something that it is not. While it is very open about the extremely unpleasant nature of its beliefs, it will often claim to be "a genuine US Patriot 2nd amendment supporter in water port of USA Floridian Oblast". Which is to say it is not Cletus from the swamp but Sergey from the farm.

Common beliefs

This troll is observed to be very vocal in its opinions on gays, women, and even darker skinned people. This explains its support of those autocratic regimes that it thinks keeps those people in their "correct" places in society – and by extension improving its own perceived role in this apparently ideal social order. As such, this troll is very supportive of Russia's invasion of Ukraine, even though in many cases it will have previously said it wouldn't happen. Once the invasion did happen, it will have confidently predicted the defeat of Ukraine within days, or at most weeks. It will also have, during 2022, relished the status of the Russian Ruble as "the best performing currency in the world".

Researchers have gathered another sign of this troll which is that it will not understand the meaning of the word "strategic" in terms of war. Rather than understanding it correctly to mean something which will irretrievably alter the course of the war (that the Kremlin insists is not a war) in Russia's favour, it believes that each of the last several destroyed piles of abandoned ruins in Eastern Ukraine were all strategic. Conversely, it will not regard Russia's retreat from Kyiv as a "strategic" defeat. It thinks that debacle was a feint.

Removal

It is unwise to discuss politics with this troll. It will enjoy your outrage and anger at its beliefs. In any case, using moral arguments against the amoral is a waste of time. In many cases, causing outrage is the sole reason for its existence. You may get some results by inauthentically believing that it is in fact a far-left troll as it can have the same beliefs as an "Anti fascist" troll. Fans of the large orange one do not enjoy, when whining about "communism in 'Merica," being told that the head of their cult has no friends besides a KGB Agent and a North Korean Stalinist.

However, it is most likely that this troll's pro-war stance is what will cause it to pollute your social media feed. If being told that The Dear Leader's fondness for KGB agents and Stalinists doesn't do it, simply mocking its inauthenticity may work. A good many of these accounts have traits that suggest they may be in the Saint Petersburg that is in Russia, not Florida, therefore mocking them for being in a warm water Oblast is effective.

Reference to previous tweets about the war not happening, the Ruble's performance, Russia's many "strategic withdrawals," "goodwill gestures" and "manoeuvrings" are also likely to irritate.

After that, a good blocking is the way forward.

Related Trolls

"Anti-fascist" troll (*Troglodytam anti fascistus*), "Anti-imperialist" troll (*Trollus anti imperiosis*).

Observations

Date seen:

Was wearing:

Distinguishing features:

Calls heard:

Other trolls it imitated:

The "Traditional values" troll.

Classic Latin: "Troglodytam homini domestica violentiam fruitur"

Vulgar Latin: "Trollus values traditional"

Basic Description

Trollologists who observe this type of troll note that it is native to a western country, tweeting about the degeneration of Western Society while extolling the "traditional values" that Russia represents. Very rarely is it spotted actually in Russia, never mind making its home there.

Since the orange one was placed above the law (in itself a completely traditional, conservative value), trollologists have noticed a new mating call of this troll, which is "your body, my choice." This is a response to those women who think that deciding who they can have sex with contravenes traditional values.

Common Beliefs

Because the West has turned away from "traditional," which is to say "Christian," values, it likes Russia because the Kremlin represents traditional, family values such as legalised wife beating, mass kidnap of children, and rape as a weapon of war.

This type of troll will also usually have the word "Christian" in their bio, perhaps accompanied by a biblical reference or quote. Never is this the one about loving your fellow man. It will also demand evidence that this week's Russian atrocity is not manufactured or a false flag. Yes, you read that correctly. A troll that believes in talking snakes and a giant wooden boat is asking you to provide evidence that it can take seriously.

Removal

Naturally, it thinks the Kremlin is a strong defender of Christian values, which is why it is bombing world heritage cathedrals in Ukraine, kidnapping thousands of children and has legalised the Christian practice of wife beating in Russia. Pointing this out to it will most likely make it turn into a "What about" troll (*Trollus quid de)*, which can be dealt with in the proscribed manner.

To the more recently devolved variation you can say that requiring that women give consent is some kind progressive idiocy bought about by the woke mind virus and that traditional values will prevent this. If you really want to flummox it, you can follow up by saying that "The Handmaid's Tale" was supposed to be a warning, not a guidebook. The troll will not have read or even heard of the book so it will not understand why it is being laughed it, and that will usually remove it. Blocking is also strongly recommended.

Finally, the mockery of its demand for evidence should be fairly straight forward. Quite why it thinks Ukraine needs to do anything after all this time to make Russia look bad is a mystery, but in the unlikely event that you get an answer that contains correctly spelled words, you will have made your own small contribution to the science of trollology.

Related Trolls

"What about" troll (*Trollus quid de*), "Short skirt" troll (*Trollus brevis lacinia*).

Observations

Date seen:

Was wearing:

Distinguishing features:

Calls heard:

Other trolls it imitated:

The "Pro business" troll.

Classic Latin: "Dicere troglodytam, qui posset deficiet varius"

Vulgar Latin: "Trollus in gratiam negotii"

Basic Description

This troll generally exists in the replies of people who think Ukraine should be given more and better weapons to defend itself. Unlike the "Defence contractors want this war" troll (*Trollus arma fabrica volunt hoc bellum*) which thinks the war is being continued because it is "good for business" and with whom it can be easily confused, this sub-species thinks the Russian invasion of Ukraine is *bad* for business and that it should stop. Often this creature will hold an elected office in a right-wing political party or be a member of a Libertarian movement.

Common Beliefs

Despite claiming in its social media bio that it is a "business owner" or being a prominent member of an allegedly pro business political party, this troll thinks being able to change international borders by force & the dismantling of the international rules-based order is good for long term economic growth.

Trollologists are currently debating the theory that in the not-too-distant future, this species of troll will have no idea at all why China got the idea that the entire of the democratic world would sit by and let it attack Taiwan, the way it did when Russia invaded Ukraine.

Removal

The inherently contradictory views of this strange creature ought to be obvious this far into the book but suggesting that its beliefs are in fact stupid and aligned with many of the "Left" trolls described so far will usually cause it great distress.

Another tactic will be to tell it that in a few short years, once the global security architecture that makes trade possible has been degraded, it will be asking why the global economy is slowing down.

While it can be easily argued that the Russian invasion of Ukraine should stop, this troll will not welcome having the obvious implications upon global business of its views explained to it if the war is stopped in the manner it suggests. Trollologists have noted that this species has not reconciled in its mind that rewarding or appeasing invasions is bad for business and makes them more likely. Also, quite why an allegedly "pro-business" troll thinks that closing Europe's largest country and its forty-five million inhabitants off entirely to western business and free market competition is somehow good for business has never been explained. That's like a builder saying the Mafia is a good for the construction industry.

When these facts are pointed out to it, it will very often morph into a "Ukraine is corrupt" (*corruptum est Ucraina*) or "Let's negotiate" trolls (*Trollus ut adferens ma. ta*).

Related Trolls

"Ukraine is corrupt" troll (*corruptum est Ucraina*), "Let's negotiate" troll *(Trollus ut adferens mandata)*.

Observations

Date seen:

Was wearing:

Distinguishing features:

Calls heard:

Other trolls it imitated:

The "Defence contractors want this war" troll.

Classic Latin: "Troglodytam auxilium tuum inimicum multas pecunias"

Vulgar Latin: "Trollus arma fabrica volunt hoc bellum"

Basic Description

A troll who thinks Russia began, and continues, this entire war merely to improve the share price of US defence contractors.

Common Beliefs

The beliefs of this troll tend to effortlessly, and shamelessly, shift just as soon as facts make something untenable. Between October 2021 and February 2022, many of these peculiar creatures were convinced that the very idea of the war was ludicrous. Prominent members of the species made comments like "there's nothing worse than the media pushing for war." In its mind, western media agencies who reported the presence of the Russian army on Ukraine's border were somehow responsible for placing them there.

Since February 2022, it believes that, because "defence contractors want this war" (that previously was not going to happen), the Kremlin decided to oblige the profits of its sworn enemy by actually invading.

Needless to say, the suggestion that Russian defence contractors might be making considerable profits from the invasion themselves is not a concept that enters the mind of this species of troll. Russia is a major, global weapons manufacturer with a weapons industry worth billions of dollars. The Kremlin is noted for its ethics in this regard and the interests of these conglomerates pay no part in formulating policy in the small minds of these trolls.

Removal

A quick search through the past posts of this creature will likely reveal contempt towards the idea of an invasion that seamlessly shifted to stating it was inevitable. Pointing this out will upset it greatly. Alongside this, pointing out the inherent contradictions and idiocies of its beliefs will, as with almost all trolls, help removal.

Related Trolls

"Ukrainians are forced to fight" troll (*trollus Ucrainorum coguntur pugnare*)

Observations

Date seen:

Was wearing:

Distinguishing features:

Calls heard:

Other trolls it imitated:

The "Ukraine is corrupt" troll.

Classic Latin: "Troglodytam cur Orci non pecunia Ucraina"

Vulgar Latin: "corruptum est Ucraina"

Basic Description

A generally right-wing troll that is usually a self-described MAGA obsessive because it hates political corruption. Yes, you read that correctly.

Common Beliefs

This troll easily believes forged evidence of Zelensky being corrupt. It also believes that instead of weapons being manufactured in the USA to replace old stock being sent to Ukraine, the US government is shipping boxes of money directly to Kyiv with which the elite there purchase extravagant lifestyles.

It believes millions and millions of Ukrainians want to fight until Russia leaves their country so that they can continue to live in a corrupt kleptocracy like Russia is.

Removal

It is not worth pointing out the endless list of political corruption allegations in the MAGA movement. Members of this cult reject the concept of facts as a liberal hoax. It will likely respond to such suggestions with some phrase that includes a variation of "the Biden crime family." At this stage, it may be worth asking why this troll thinks that Joe Biden is simultaneously senile AND a criminal mastermind at the centre of a web corrupt international finance. The fact that the orange order appointed judges declared Biden to be above the law will not enter its head anyway.

The simplest question to ask of this creature is why, if Zelensky is so shamelessly corrupt, Russia does not just bribe him – an approach that would surely be cheaper than the invasion is. It will then move to becoming a "What about" troll (*trollus quid de*) and you can deal with it accordingly.

Related Trolls

"Defence contractors want this war" troll (*Trollus arma fabrica volunt hoc bellum*), "MAGA" troll *(Trollus Russia et iterum maga).*

Observations

Date seen:

Was wearing:

Distinguishing features:

Calls heard:

Other trolls it imitated:

The "This is a proxy war" troll.

Classic Latin: "Troglodytam ineundo bellum in quo Orci procuratorem obtinere oblitus est"

Vulgar Latin: "Trollus hoc bellum innuendo"

Basic Description

Rather than being unprovoked invasion aimed at regime change launched by an imperialist power, this troll thinks the entire war in Ukraine is a proxy war started by the USA.

Common Beliefs

The troll thinks that the USA intends to fight Russia to the last Ukrainian, thus, this is a proxy war. Sadly, it seems that the Kremlin forgot to get Russia a proxy. But to this troll, it is still a proxy war. The idea that Russia might itself be little more than a proxy of Iran and North Korea as they fight the USA to the last Russian is a concept that will not enter its head.

Removal

Aside from reminding it that Putin, despite being such a master strategist, seems to have forgotten to have got himself a proxy, it is worth reversing the troll's own arguments to point out that Iran and North Korea appear to be fighting Ukraine to the last Russian. Reducing a supposed "Great Power" like Russia to a mere proxy of countries like this will irritate it greatly. After laughing at it, you should block it.

Related Trolls

"Ukrainians are forced to fight" troll (*trolls Ucrainorum coguntur pugnare*)

Observations

Date seen:

Was wearing:

Distinguishing features:

Calls heard:

Other trolls it imitated:

The "Ukrainians are forced to fight" troll.

Classic Latin: "Troglodytam Ucrainorum nullam habent potestatem super quos pugnant"

Vulgar Latin: "Trollus Ucrainorum coguntur pugnare"

Basic Description

A troll that will appear in your timeline making some variation of the claim that Ukrainians do not want this war, in as much as they are being duped into thinking Russia is their enemy by the "mainstream media."

Common Beliefs

A troll that believes that Ukraine, as soon as it is deprived of western weapons, will immediately welcome their Russian liberators as brothers that they will suddenly feel compelled to embrace.

The entire concept of this troll's beliefs relies on some serious mental gymnastics, even by the standards of trolls. Scientists who study trolls in their native environments are undecided if this sub-species of troll believes Ukraine's continued fight against Russia is a result in some kind of massive mind control system, or because Ukrainians are being pressed into war against their will, despite the fact their soldiers have the weapons to resist the people who are apparently forcing them.

Removal

Simply stating that the idea that after over two years ordinary Ukrainians are being forced to fight is absurd is usually enough to cause this troll to transmogrify into one of its related trolls, which can be dealt with the in the proscribed manner.

Related Trolls

"This is a proxy war" troll *(Trollus hoc bellum innuendo)*

Observations

Date seen:

Was wearing:

Distinguishing features:

Calls heard:

Other trolls it imitated:

The "Why don't you go fight yourself" troll.

Classic Latin: "Melioris argumenti cogitare non possum quod non sum valde captiosus"

Vulgar Latin: "Ego non perniciosasque impetus aut iungere"

Basic Description

This troll will most likely appear in your timeline if you are making the argument that Ukraine should be given more means with which to defend itself. It will feel smug and confident in the belief that it will have come up with an unbeatable argument. Needless to say, this far into the book, you now know it has not.

Common Beliefs

Such trolls often believe that somehow they will one day be asked to fight for Ukraine themselves and that (at the time of writing) thousands of Western soldiers are already there. This will be revealed when the many mothers whose sons really have died in Ukraine begin to protest against this secret operation by western governments that sent their children to die.

It can also be the case that numerous types of usually right spectrum trolls, when confronted with mockery, shapeshift into this form of troll, thinking that they have finally won a debate.

Removal

Removal is fairly simple. You can ask it why it does not go join a suicidal meat wave assault if it wants Russia to win so much, since it seems to think the only option to helping the victim defend itself it is to physically take part in combat. It will doubtless decline the offer but point out that "Ukraine is having to grab men off the street" in order to sustain the war. It will have no memory of the 300,000 people who fled Russia when the Kremlin announced the mobilisation it denied would happen.

Unpleasant forms of this troll may appear to delight in Ukraine's misery and post clips of graves of dead Ukrainians. Recalling that trolls enjoy outrage, rather than be angered you should mock this by saying you are convinced also that Russia has sustained just three minor casualties in advancing at a snail's pace for nearly 3 years against NATO's 9-foot-tall cyborgs. After this you should block it and get on with your life.

Related Trolls

"Ukraine is forced to fight" troll (*Trollus Ucrainorum coguntur pugnare*), "This is a proxy war" troll (*Trollus hoc bellum innuendo*).

Observations

Date seen:

Was wearing:

Distinguishing features:

Calls heard:

Other trolls it imitated:

The "Let's negotiate" troll.

Classic Latin: "Troglodytam liberalis cum aliis in terries"

Vulgar Latin: "Trollus ut adferens mandata"

Basic Description

Meet a troll that wants to negotiate to end the Russian invasion of Ukraine but on Russia's terms, obviously. It believes that this deal, finally, is actually the deal Russia will stick to.

Common Beliefs

It believes that there is a simple deal that can end this war on terms that everyone will find reasonable. And by everyone, it means Russia.

Removal

This troll has not noticed that Russia has said it will not negotiate. It also thinks that despite the fact that Russia has not honoured the UN Charter, the Nuclear Non-Proliferation treaty, the Helsinki accords, the Belovezha accords, the Budapest Memorandum, The Black Sea Treaty, The Russia-Ukraine Friendship Treaty, the Treaty of the Azov Sea and Kerch Strait, the Russia Ukraine Border Treaty and the Kharkiv Pact, this next proposed treaty is the one that Russia will definitely honour.

Pointing out that despite the rather long list of treaties Russia has violated, being convinced this one will work is idiocy will often silence your troll. You may wish to sarcastically mention that appeasement has a long history of always being a sound policy in international relations. Should it then mention the Minsk Agreements, you can remind it that they were only needed as Russia couldn't honour the list already mentioned and then ask when Russia returned to Ukraine its eastern border via the "rebels" it didn't have anything to do with, as you will learn about later.

Having previously been seen as a left spectrum troll, it has recently been reclassified by trollologists to being in the right-wing spectrum. This is due to the fact that a certain orange troll thought it could negotiate an end to the Russian invasion of Ukraine in a day. Right wing trolls think that a problem with socialism is that you eventually run out other people's money. The "Let's negotiate" trolls, despite often being very right wing, do not know that with appeasement you eventually run out other people's countries. Still, no one has ever accused them of being smart.

Related Trolls

"This will cause a nuclear war" troll (*Trollus hoc faciam bellum nuclei*), "Pro-Business" troll (*Trollus in gratiam negotii*).

Observations

Date seen:

Was wearing:

Distinguishing features:

Calls heard:

Other trolls it imitated:

The "MAGA" troll.

Classic Latin: "Troglodytam damnatus felo aurantiaco"

Vulgar Latin: "Trollus Russia et iterum maga"

Basic Description

A very common specimen indeed, this troll often is a "genuine US patriot 2nd amendment protect south border won't vote for Iosef Bidenovich" that is oddly interested in Ruble's exchange rate to the US Dollar.

Authentic American versions of this troll have a curious and amusing trait that is easy to observe. If you are to tell it that its great orange god is lying (as it does whenever it speaks), it is almost certain that it will respond by laughing at your apparent frustration at being lied to. When you point out that its cult leader is lying not only to you, but to it as well, the "MAGA" troll will express confusion but essentially be content to receive lies that comfort it, rather than facts which upset it, provided it can believe you are upset at being lied too as well.

Common Beliefs

Inauthentic trolls pretending to be American believe that anything that is bad for Ukraine is good.

Trolls who actually are in the USA believe anything they are told by their orange god. They do not trust the "mainstream media" and claim to be "free thinkers." Despite this, "MAGA" trolls all believe the same thing. That same thing might be exactly the opposite of what they were told to believe yesterday.

Removal

It often completely pointless to debate with this troll for three reasons. Firstly, it may well be run by an employee of a troll farm. Secondly, these trolls are often automated accounts sent to promote outrage. Thirdly, if it is not either of these and is an actual MAGA fan then it is a waste of time debating with morons who get their own opinions *and* their own facts.

Should you identify it as either of the first two, you can signal to the troll farm that runs it that you will not take abuse lying down by mocking its absurd grammar. Following this, blocking is the best option.

If it is actually a "MAGA" troll that really likes the Kremlin and supports Russia's invasion of Ukraine, you can amuse yourself but pointing out that the orange one is a closet communist due to his infatuation with Stalinists and KGB agents.

A final method is to note that "MAGA" trolls are fond of pointing out that "facts don't care about your feelings," which is a strange contradiction given their preference for the comforting lies mentioned above. Observations have shown they tend to become intellectually paralysed or morph into another troll described in this book when this is pointed out to them.

Related Trolls

"Fascist" troll (*Trollus favens fascistus*), "Tech/crypto bro" troll (*Trollus Lorem secretum monetæ*), "Pro-business" troll (*Trollus in gratiam negotii*).

Observations

Date seen:

Was wearing:

Distinguishing features:

Calls heard:

Other trolls it imitated:

The "Tech/crypto bro" troll.

Classic Latin: "Troglodytam nolens celibat stultus"

Vaulgar Latin: "Trollus Lorem secretum monetæ"

Basic Description

Of all the trolls that have revealed themselves since February 2022, the fact that the "Tech-bro/crypto bro" trolls are often very pro-Russia might be the one that has surprised trollologists the most. If ever there was a troll that "believes the opposite of the current thing," it is the "Tech/crypto bro" troll.

Common Beliefs

One of the earliest times this set of trolls really appeared in great number was when Ukraine was about to be given western tanks. This previously rather rare troll species noticed that the Lord High Crypto Bro had decided that tanks were death traps on the battlefield, unlikely to make a difference and thus a waste of time. It simultaneously believed these tanks, that were deadly to their operators and that would make no difference, to also be an escalation towards World War 3. It never stopped to ask itself why, if the tanks were such pointless menaces to their users, did Russia object to Ukraine being given them, or why Russia itself possesses so many of them itself.

You can learn a lot about this species by observing who they follow and who they retweet. It is near ubiquitous for trolls of this type that take an interest in matters outside online gaming to retweet American commentors on the war who make astonishingly bad predictions that are always wrong, and who frequently are also convicted paedophiles. It is also quite likely that this troll will be excessively attentive to female, pro-Russian bloggers in the vain hope they might be the first female to ever have sex with them. The final trait to observe is that at some stage during 2022 and up to the first half of 2023 this troll will have tweeted something to the effect of "The Ruble is the best performing currency in the world".

Removal

After pointing out the inconsistencies in their arguments hinted at above, a response this troll does not like is to be told that the Venn diagram of people who retweet sex offenders, claim that the Ruble is doing really well & Kremlin apologists is a perfect circle.

Another tactic that may work is to modify their argument that crypto currency is a better investment than diamonds (or any asset that is not a scarcity of nothing) because diamonds can be smashed by a sledgehammer, but non-fungible token (NFT) currency can never be destroyed. Thus, you can suggest that they invent a new NFT called a "Non-Fungible Tank" so that it can never be destroyed either. The idea makes as much sense as they do.

Related Trolls

"Pro-business" troll (*Trollus in gratiam negotii*), "Fascist" troll (*Trollus favens fascistus*).

Observations

Date seen:

Was wearing:

Distinguishing features:

Calls heard:

Other trolls it imitated:

The "Genocide in the Donbas" troll.

Classic Latin: "Troglodytam boum excretium artifex genocidia in Donbas"

Vulgar Latin: "Trollus genocidia in Donbas"

Basic Description

Trollologists are divided about whether this troll aims to explain Russia or to excuse it. All trolls believe that Russia is the victim so this one, a close relative of the "What about" troll (*Trollus quid de*), will come out of hiding whenever there is an atrocity committed by Russia and say, "Russia had to stop the genocide in the Donbas".

This used to be an exclusively left troll but in recent years, it has attracted right wing trolls as well. This is usually because the latter are attracted to the idea of preventing a genocide against white people, even if, like in the Donbas it has made up, as opposed to one against darker people that is not, for example in the former Yugoslavia. Oddly, preventing a fake genocide against one set of European people by inflicting a real genocide on other Europeans is concept it will struggle with.

Common Beliefs

This troll believes that from 2014 until 2022, "pro-Russian rebels", who had absolutely nothing to do with Russia, but who shared a border with Russia, fought Ukraine with unlimited Russian ammunition, Russian spare parts, Russian fuel, Russian soldiers, and Russian propaganda to prevent "genocide in the Donbas".

Considering this, this species believes it logical that Russia should invade and completely flatten all of Eastern Ukraine and kill tens to hundreds of thousands of civilians in order to help the "pro Russians" (who had nothing to do with Russia) get Ukraine to stop not doing that.

Removal

Quite why this troll thinks the Kremlin cares about its "compatriots abroad," given what it did to its compatriots at home in either of the Chechen wars, is easy to explain. Trolls do not think and are angered by the prospect of having to. Furthermore, in a characteristic shared somewhat with the "CIA coup" troll (*Trollus media intelligentia res propellente*), it will believe that Chechens are just different enough that it doesn't matter if a few hundred thousand of them are killed in the name of the multi-polar world. Therefore, asking it to explain how Russia never interferes abroad in other countries but somehow the pro Russian rebels were so well equipped will make it shape shift into another form of troll.

You may recall that in the summer of 2023 Evgeny Prigozhin (if you can remember that pro western, neo-con, CIA asset) did say that Russia's claim about "genocide in the Donbas" was complete rubbish. You can always ask this kind of troll to ask him about the topic. Except it cannot because shortly after Prigozhin said this the former leader of Wagner found out "what air defense was doing?" and died of extreme altitude cancer.

Related Trolls

"CIA coup" troll *(Trollus media intelligentia res propellente)*

Observations

Date seen:

Was wearing:

Distinguishing features:

Calls heard:

Other trolls it imitated:

Certificate

Congratulations on completing the book. Once you have completed the observations of all the species of troll in the wild, you are a fully qualified Trollologist and can spot and remove all these types of trolls seen online. Below is a handy certificate to prove your achievement. Feel free to fill it in yourself and hang it proudly for all to see. You worked hard and earned it!

Do not forget what Darth said in the foreword! If you tag him in a picture of this, he may just arrange an antidote for you.

CERTIFICATE OF TRAINING

This certifies that

_____

has successfully completed the Darth Putin KGB training to become a certified trollologist

Darth Putin KGB
Darth Putin KGB

_____
Date

Author's note.

As with the book "How to Tankie," this book grew out of a thread of tweets which went viral when I made a list of the different types of trolls who appear in Darth's timeline. While most of the comments were very positive, often by people remarking that they had seen a particular type of troll many times, I knew I was onto something when some of the trolls themselves were particularly angered by it.

I decided to turn the thread into a book as I felt putting it together in this format might help people understand the absurdities that trolls believe and thus learn to not just be stationary targets for the fake outrage and ethics, as well as the discord and division, these people/bots peddle. While I will never know for sure, the fact that Darth will swing back at trolls does seem to reduce the amount of attention He gets from the troll farms. In fact, Darth is blocked by numerous Russian embassies, "diplomats," media agencies, the Foreign Ministry, and the former Russian President. I suspect that this is because reducing their arguments to their basic components in Darth's style undermines and subverts the message they are trying to put out. The last thing they want is for online collectives, for example, to be given a free lesson in how to laugh at their narratives and ruin their replies. Darth operates by the rule that if a troll draws a verbal sword against the Czar, it should throw away the scabbard. It appears to be effective.

Conversely, I have observed that the people who do not swing back tend to become more popular targets for the trolls and their leaders. This is truer for those who show that trolling upsets them. This mirrors the real world, where if you do not impose a cost on the Kremlin for its actions, it will keep doing them. This is not to diminish the real distress sustained trolling can cause, but I honestly believe amused contempt followed by making them irrelevant by blocking will help.

I am not intending to suggest that you will always get the last word with a troll or that you should try. Darth also operates by the rule of "mock and block." If you treat a troll like a someone else's unwashed, unpleasant child who says something mean about you when you walk past a playpark, you are well on your way to a more agreeable social media experience. Does it honestly matter if a 5-year-old says your shoes are stupid? Does it matter what an incel in his mother's basement says either? No. But the latter is an adult who you can mock guilt-free.

A lot of troll accounts are run by people who feel validated by receiving attention, even if it is in the form of scathing mockery. Darth's experience is that some of them are almost certainly run by troll farms intended to sow outrage and division. By mocking them, an account of Darth's size can influence others with good ways to respond to their attacks. For example, when Navalny was killed, numerous trolls attempted to justify his probable murder and previous torture by releasing edited videos of him attending far right rallies in

Russia where large groups of people were giving Nazi salutes. Whatever one thinks of Navalny's opinions, by mocking these trolls as idiots for highlighting how serious Russia's problem with the far right actually is, Darth was able to furnish people who do not pay as close attention to Russia as He does with an argument with which to laugh at trolls. Again, while I will never know for sure, Darth never again saw this justification for Navalny's death being pushed at any scale. Indeed, the accounts that pushed it were immediately flooded with the Kremlin's own narratives to justify its invasion of Ukraine being thrown back them.

While this book is presented in a satirical style, I believe the message is serious. If you laugh at the trolls for the inconsistencies, hypocrisies, and idiocies of their arguments, you will find social media a lot easier. If after this, you just block them as you might that child, you will also be better off.

Darth Putin KGB, November 2024.

Printed in Poland
by Amazon Fulfillment
Poland Sp. z o.o., Wrocław